ABCs Affirmation

Positive Affirmations For Toddlers + Up

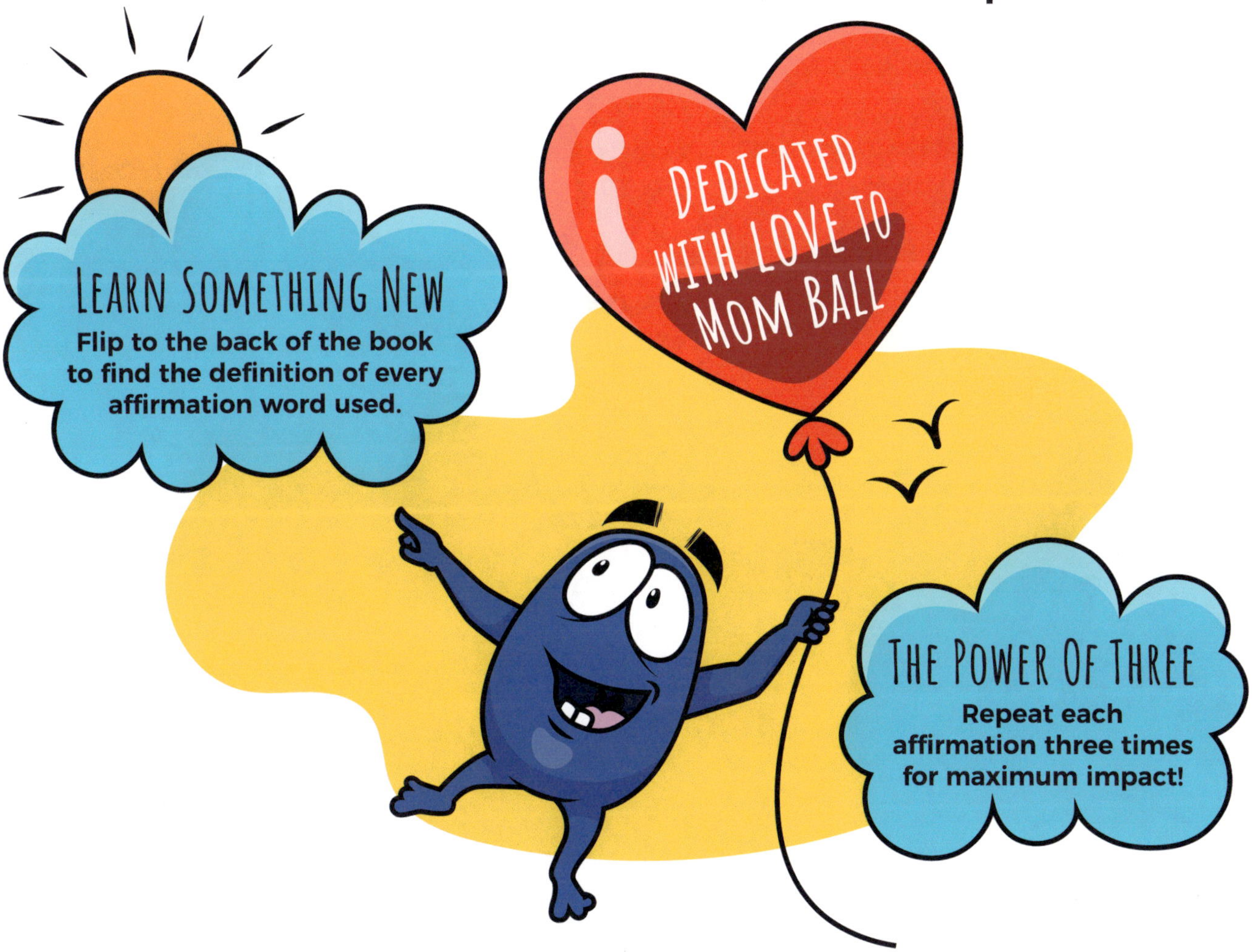

Learn Something New
Flip to the back of the book to find the definition of every affirmation word used.

Dedicated with Love to Mom Ball

The Power Of Three
Repeat each affirmation three times for maximum impact!

Written by Dave W. Ball
Illustrated by Design Pickle

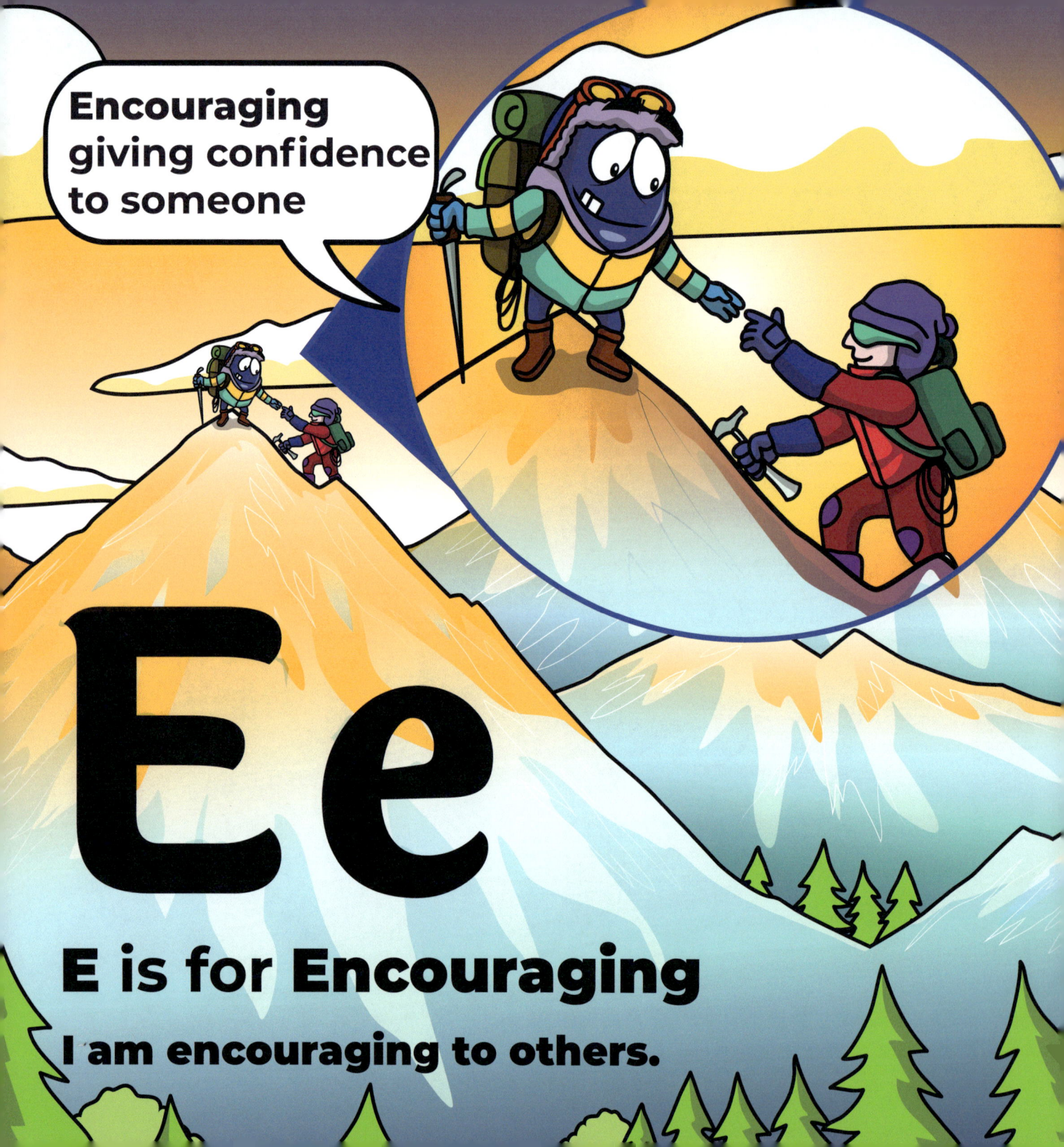

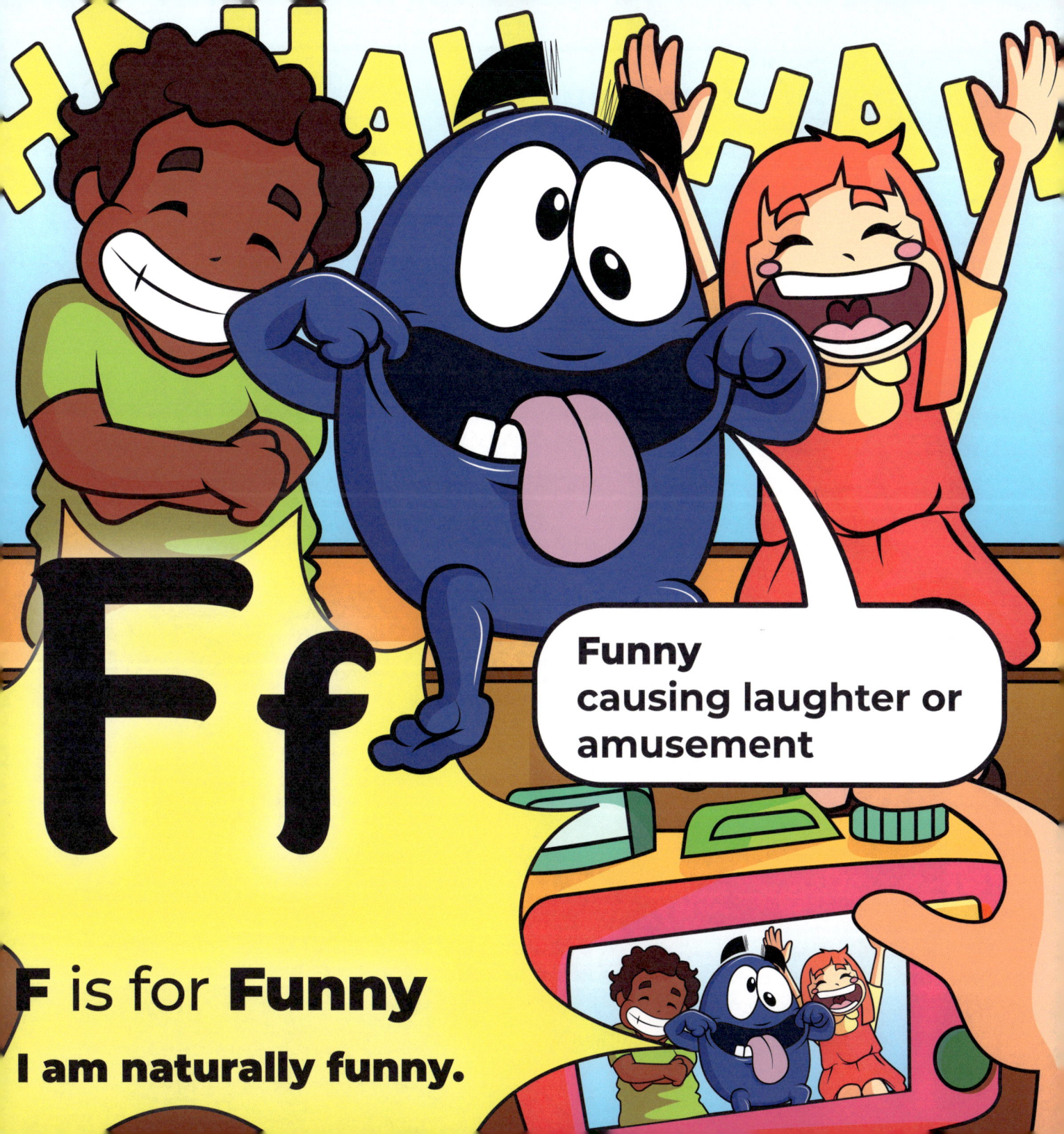

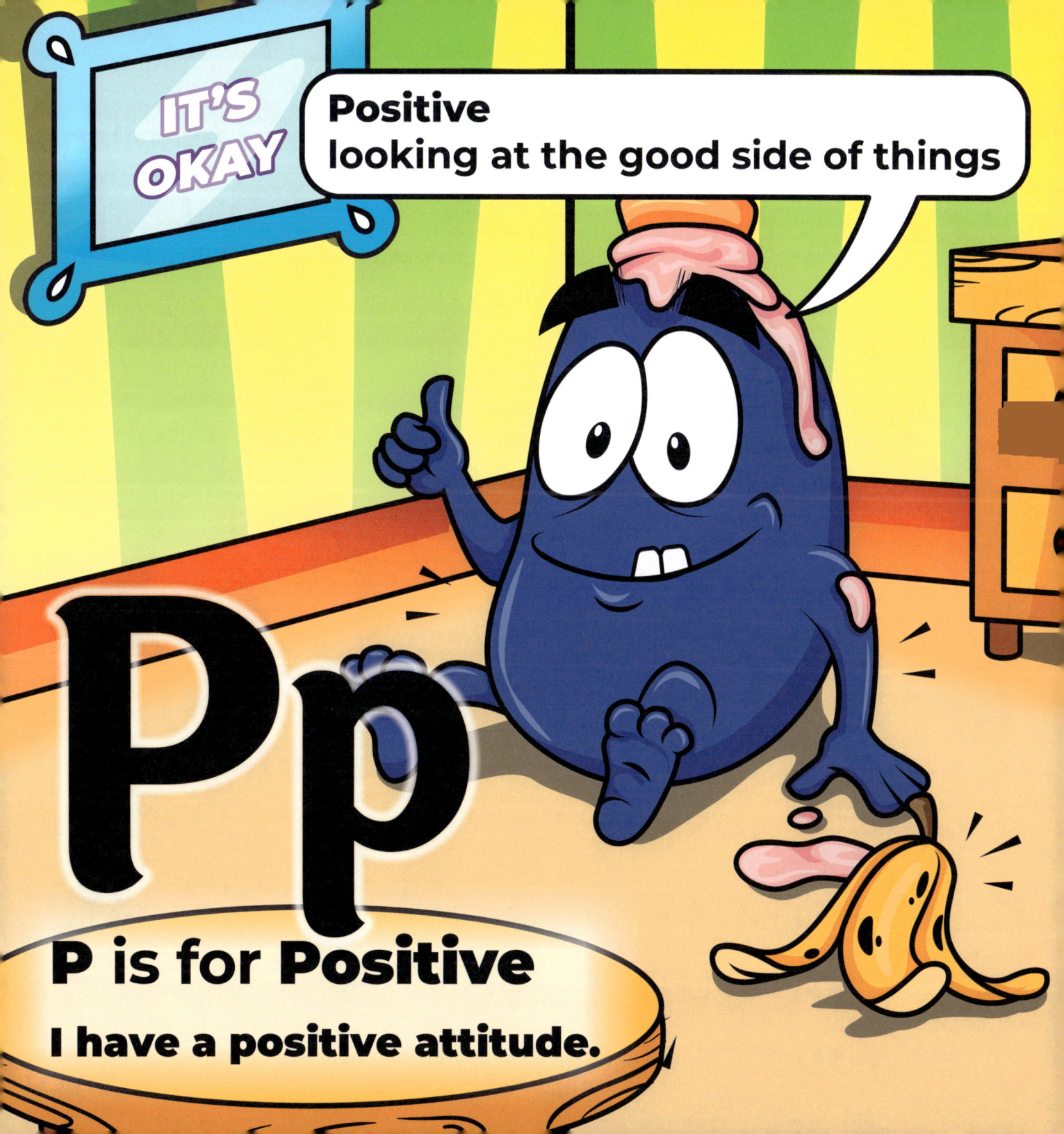

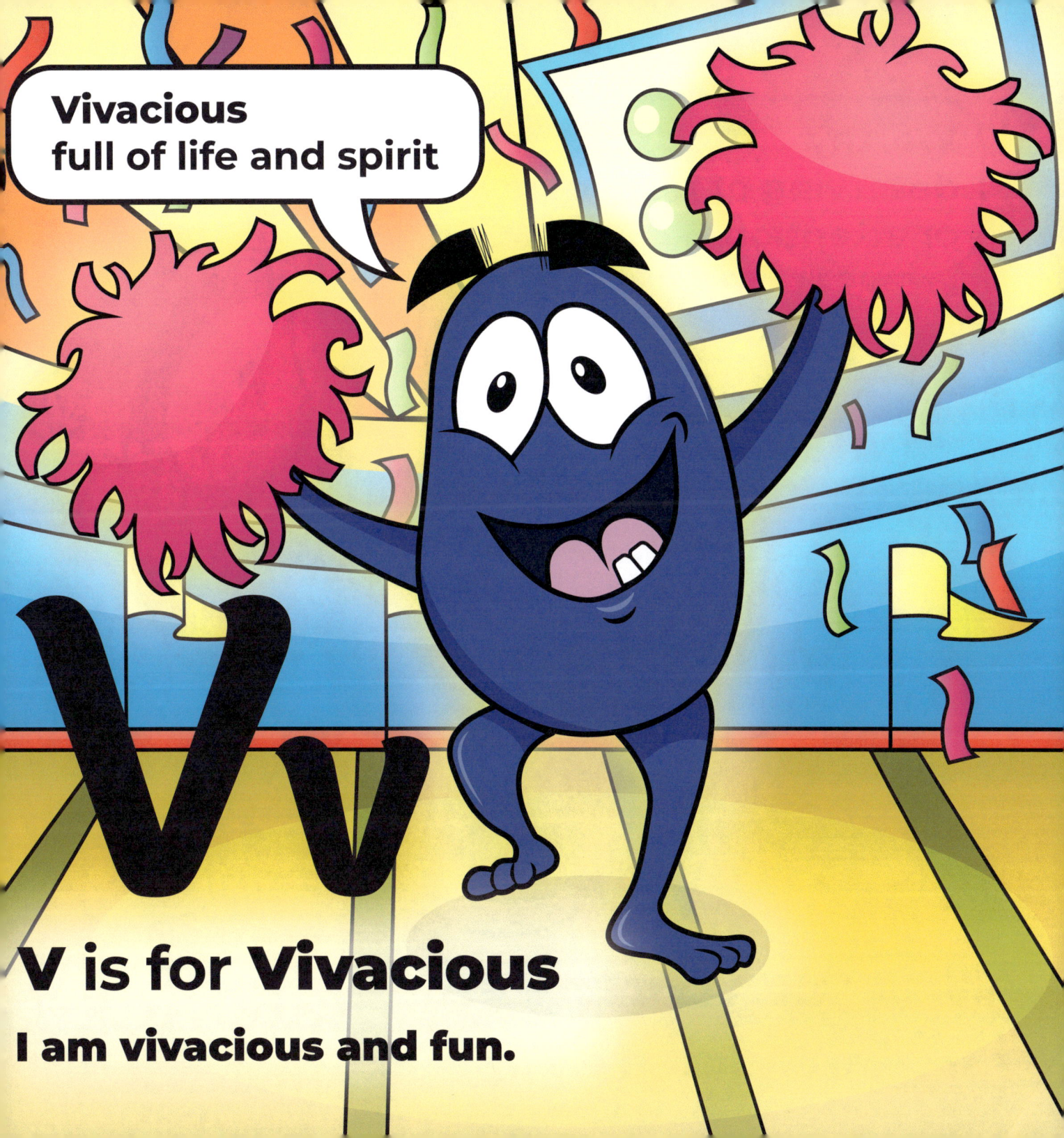

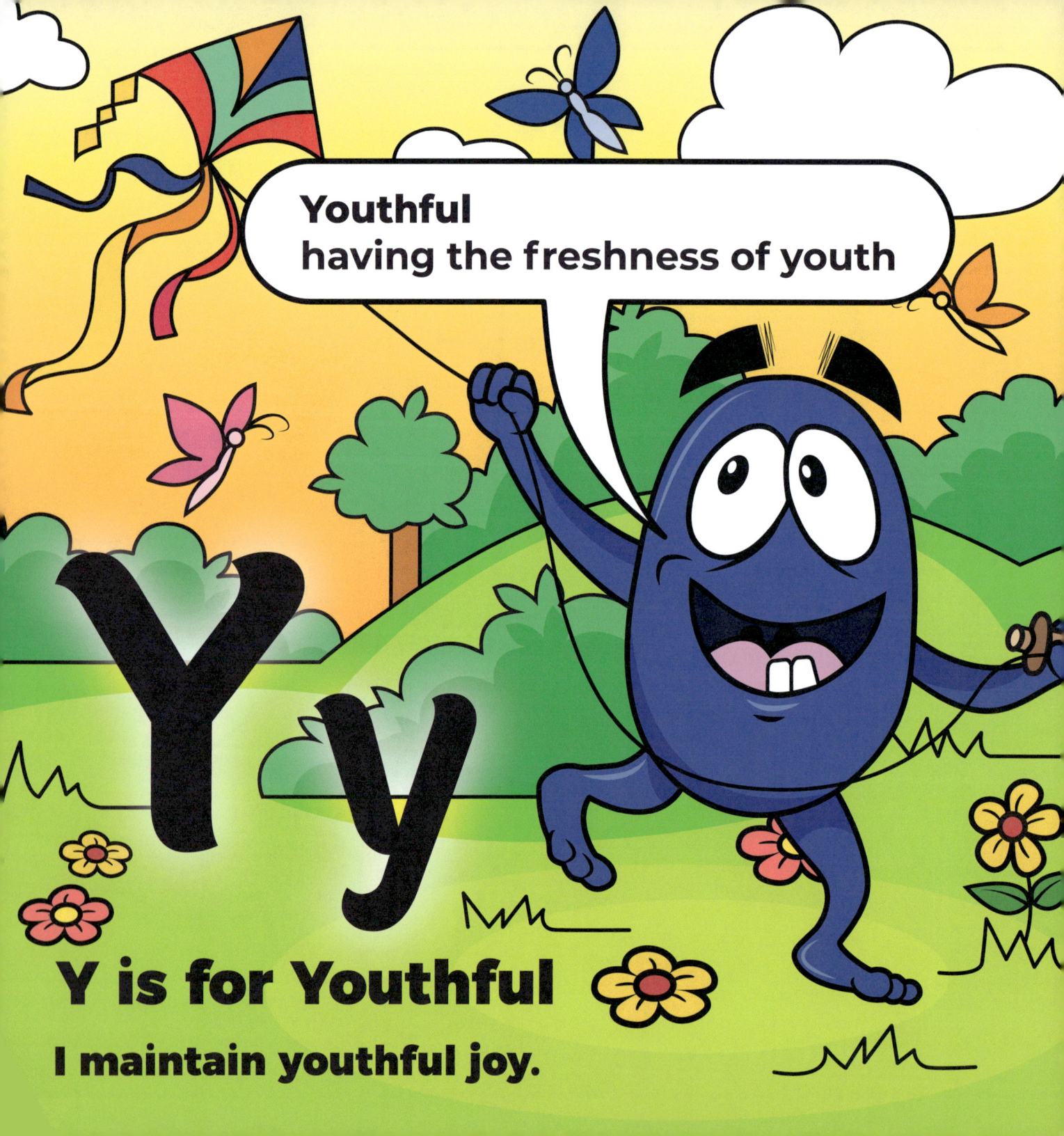

Turn Hiccups Into Smiles With The Hiccups Series

SCAN ME

Copyright ©2021 Dave W. Ball. All rights reserved. First printing, 2021.
ISBN: 978-1-7344656-1-7 (Paperback)
info@primerhymekidsbooks.com
www.prkb.com

GLOSSARY

Achieve
getting by means of hard work

Believe
accepting as true

Creative
using imagination to invent new things

Dependable
deserving trust or confidence

Encouraging
giving confidence to someone

Funny
causing laughter or amusement

Generous
willing to give or share

Honest
being truthful in what we say and do

Innovative
introducing or using new ideas or methods

Jubilant
expressing great joy

Kind
bringing happiness to others

Legendary
being well-known or famous

Meaningful
having value or purpose

Noble
having courage and honesty

Optimistic
hopeful for positive outcomes

Positive
looking at the good side of things

Quality
high value or excellence

Respectful
being polite and having manners

Stupendous
amazing or awesome

Truth
the real facts about something

Unique
one of a kind

Vivacious
full of life and spirit

Worthy
deserving of respect or attention

X-Factor
strong but unpredictable influence

Youthful
having the freshness of youth

Zealous
energetic desire to get something done

AFFIRMATIONS

A is for Achieve
Whatever I dream for myself, I achieve.

B is for Believe
I believe in myself.

C is for Creative
I am effortlessly creative.

D is for Dependable
I am dependable and resourceful.

E is for Encouraging
I am encouraging to others.

F is Funny
I am naturally funny.

G is for Generous
I am a generous giver.

H is for Honest
I am always honest.

I is for Innovative
I am an innovative problem solver.

J is for Jubilant
I am jubilant.

K is for Kind
I am kind.

L is for Legendary
The positive impact I make on the world is legendary;

M is for Meaningful
My friendships are supportive and meaningful.

N is for Noble
I am noble and strong.

O is for Optimistic
I choose to feel optimistic.

P is for Positive
I have a positive attitude.

Q is for Quality
I am grateful for quality time with my family.

R is for Respectful
I am respectful and considerate at all times.

S is for Stupendous
I am a stupendous learner.

T is for Truth
I always tell the truth.

U is for Unique
I am unique and talented.

V is for Vivacious
I am vivacious and fun.

W is for Worthy
I am worthy just the way I am.

X is for X-Factor
I am the x-factor.

Y is for Youthful
I maintain youthful joy.

Z is for Zealous
I am zealous about helping others.

Made in United States
Troutdale, OR
05/11/2024